Rainy Day Surprises
YOU CAN MAKE

Written by Robyn Supraner   Illustrated by Renzo Barto

Troll Associates

Library of Congress Cataloging in Publication Data

Supraner, Robyn.
 Rainy day surprises you can make.

 SUMMARY: Directions for making a pencil holder,
elephant, castle, barrette, sock puppet, and other
projects.
 1. Handicraft—Juvenile literature. [1. Handi-
craft] I. Barto, Renzo. II. Title.
TT160.S93   745.5   80-19858
ISBN 0-89375-428-5
ISBN 0-89375-429-3 (pbk.)

Copyright © 1981 by Troll Associates, Mahwah, New Jersey.

10 9 8 7 6 5 4

CONTENTS

FINGERPRINT PAINTINGS

Fingerprint paintings are easy and fun to make.

Here's what you need:

Poster paints

Paper

Felt-tip pens
(It is helpful to have a damp washcloth nearby.)

Here's what you do:

1 Put a small dab of paint on the tip of your finger.

Spread the paint to make it even.

2 Press down on a piece of paper so you leave a fingerprint. If the print looks too heavy, wipe some of the paint off your

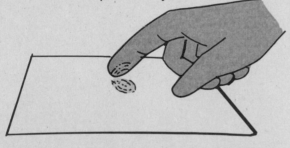

finger before you print again. (*Note:* Use your thumb for larger prints and your pinkie for smaller ones.)

3 Wipe your fingers clean with a damp washcloth when you've finished making prints.

4 Fill in the details of the painting with a felt-tip pen.

Some good subjects for fingerprint paintings are rabbits, butterflies, flowers, trees, fish, and birds. You can make a beautiful peacock with different colored paints. Use fingerprint paintings to decorate greeting cards and party invitations. Put a painting on top of your stationery. Print one on the seal of an envelope. On the following pages are some ideas you may want to try. Or create some designs of your own!

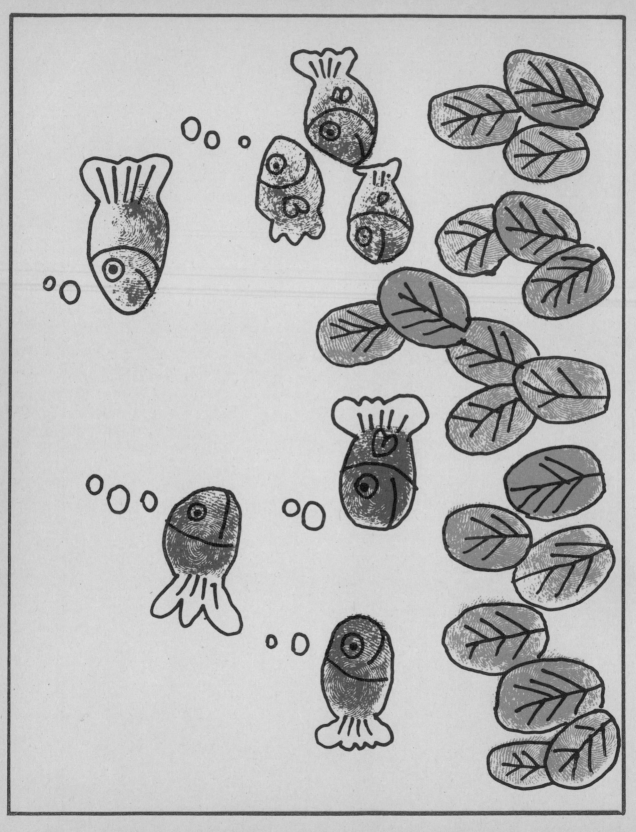

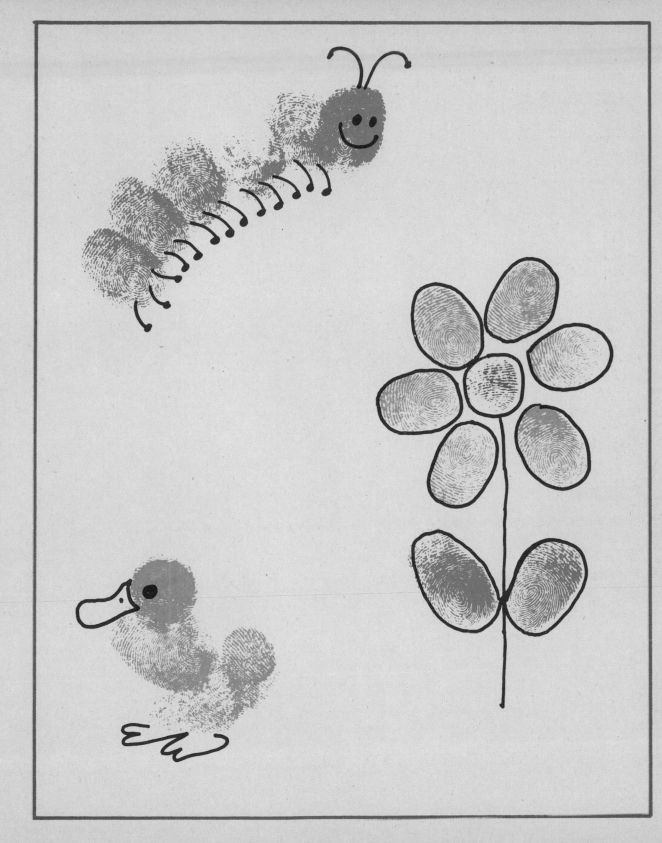

EASY PENCIL HOLDER

Here's what you need:

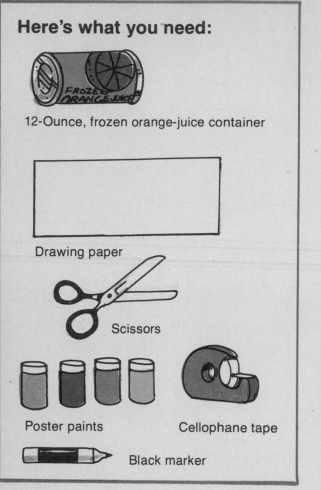

12-Ounce, frozen orange-juice container

Drawing paper

Scissors

Poster paints   Cellophane tape

Black marker

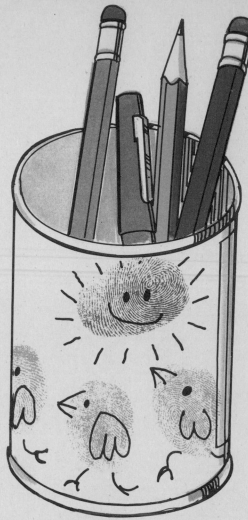

Here's what you do:

1   Cut a piece of drawing paper to fit around the juice container.

2   Make a mother hen and her chicks with fingerprint paintings. Use your thumb for the hen's body. Use your second finger for her head. Use your pinkie to make the chicks. Make the sun with your thumb.

3 Use a black marker to finish the picture.

4 Wrap the picture around the juice container and tape it.

Extra:

Glue strips of colored paper around the top and bottom of the container. Cover the finished pencil holder with a coat of clear white shellac.

CROCODILE CLIP

Here's what you need:

Wooden clothespin
(the kind with a spring)

Paints and brush

Toothpick

Glass

Clear nail polish

Here's what you do:

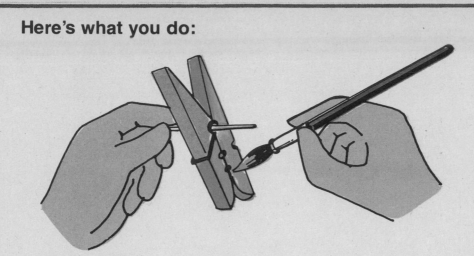

1 Paint a wooden clothespin. Green is a good color for a crocodile, but you may use any color you like.

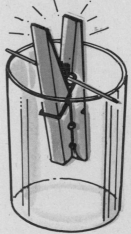

2 Stick a toothpick through the clothespin's spring. Rest the toothpick across the mouth of a glass. Let the clothespin hang in the glass to dry.

3 Paint the crocodile's eyes and nose. Paint a crocodile design on its back. When the eyes are dry, paint an orange dot in the center of each one.

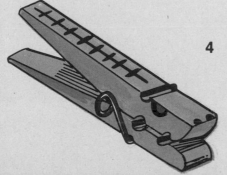

4 Brush on a coat of clear nail polish for a smooth and shiny finish. Keep your crocodile clip on your desk to hold important papers. Or use it as a clipboard. Make two, and give one as a gift! Crocodile clips also make good puppets.

ELEPHANT

Here's what you need:

Brown or gray
construction
paper

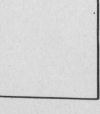

White paper

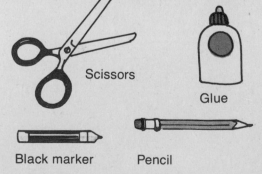

Scissors

Glue

Black marker

Pencil

Here's what you do:

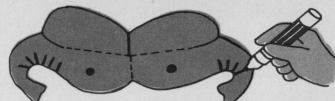

1   Fold a piece of brown or gray construction paper in half.

2   Using the patterns on the next two pages, draw the elephant's body and its head on the construction paper. The elephant's back must lie along the fold.

3   Cut out the elephant.

4   On each side of the elephant's head, use a black marker to draw an eye and the folds of the elephant's trunk. Draw toenails on the feet of the elephant.

5   Glue both sides of the elephant's head and trunk together. Fold out the ears.

6   Bend the two tabs on the elephant's belly and glue them together.

7   Cut two tusks out of white paper, using the pattern on the next page. Glue a tusk to each side of the elephant's head.

8   Place the elephant's head over its shoulders and glue together.

Extra:

To make the elephant's eyes sparkle, dip the point of a toothpick into white paint. Put a dot of paint in the center of each eye.

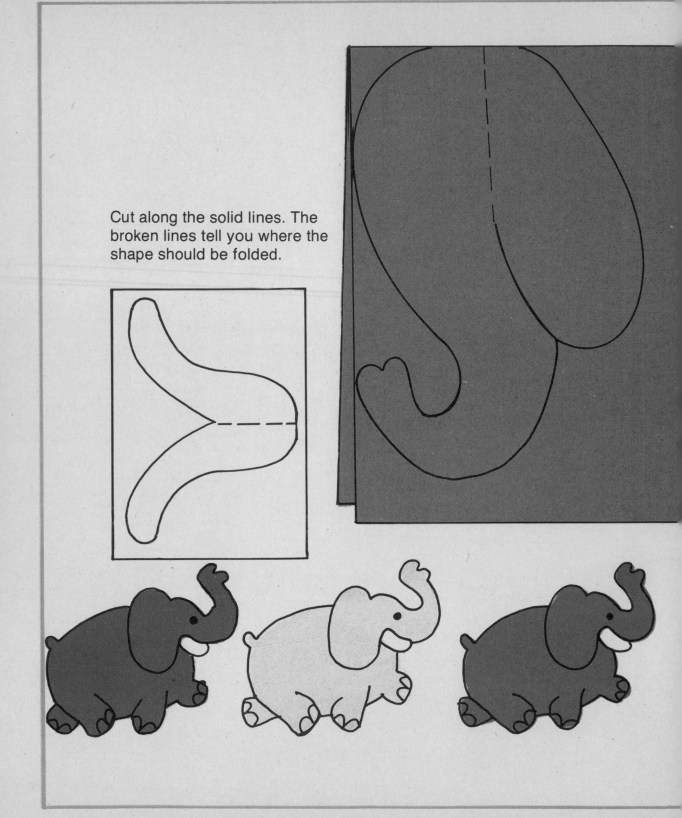

Cut along the solid lines. The broken lines tell you where the shape should be folded.

PEANUT-IN-THE-CUP TOY

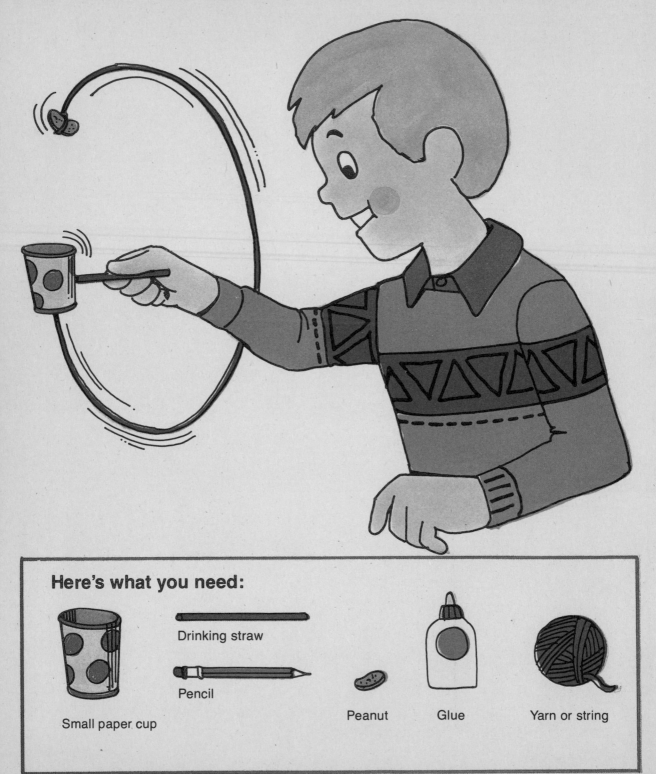

Here's what you need:

Small paper cup

Drinking straw

Pencil

Peanut

Glue

Yarn or string

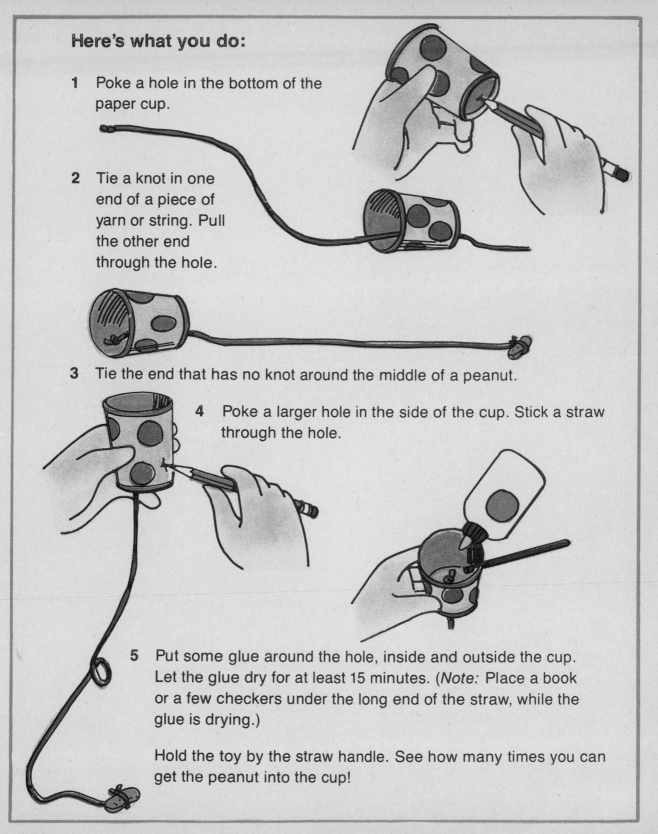

Here's what you do:

1   Poke a hole in the bottom of the paper cup.

2   Tie a knot in one end of a piece of yarn or string. Pull the other end through the hole.

3   Tie the end that has no knot around the middle of a peanut.

4   Poke a larger hole in the side of the cup. Stick a straw through the hole.

5   Put some glue around the hole, inside and outside the cup. Let the glue dry for at least 15 minutes. (*Note:* Place a book or a few checkers under the long end of the straw, while the glue is drying.)

Hold the toy by the straw handle. See how many times you can get the peanut into the cup!

Here's what you need:

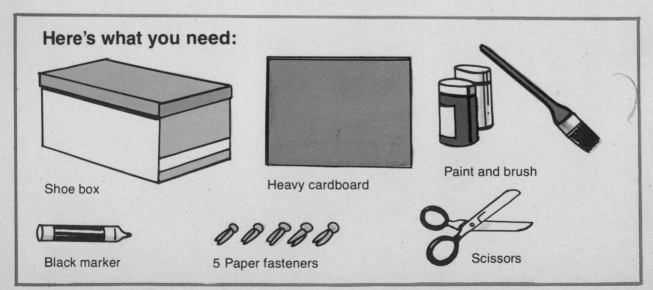

Shoe box

Heavy cardboard

Paint and brush

Black marker

5 Paper fasteners

Scissors

Here's what you do:

1 Paint a shoe box red.
This is the wagon.

2 Using the cardboard, cut
four circles for the wheels
and a T-shape for the handle.

3 Paint the handle black.

4 With the black marker, draw spokes
and a rim on each wheel.

5 Make a hole in the center of each wheel. Attach two wheels to each side
of the wagon, using the paper fasteners. Make a hole at the base of the
T-shaped handle and attach it to the bottom of the wagon.

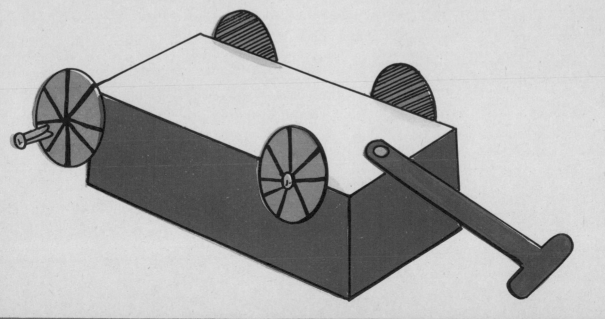

BABY CARRIAGE

Turn the wagon into a baby carriage:

1 Cut off one end of the shoe box cover.

2 Make a cut in each side of the cover. In the picture, the solid lines are to be cut.

3 Fold the cover along the dotted line. Use a staple to hold it in place.

4 Paint it red or blue. When it is dry, you can decorate it and the wagon with white flowers. Staple the top to the bottom of the carriage.

5 Cut out a long strip of cardboard. Paint it black on both sides. Bend it in a U-shape. This is the carriage's handle. Staple it to the front of the baby carriage.

CHOCOLATE BANANA POPS

Do you like chocolate? Do you like bananas?
If you do, you'll love these pops!

Here's what you need:

Spoon

Knife

Plate

2 Bananas

Wax paper

3 Tablespoons cocoa

COCOA

½ Teaspoon vanilla extract

4 Popsicle sticks

1 Tablespoon milk

2 Tablespoons honey

Here's what you do:

1. Mix the honey, cocoa, milk, and vanilla on a plate. Stir the mixture until it is smooth.

2. Peel the bananas. Cut them in half. Push a popsicle stick into each cut end.

3. Roll the banana halves in the cocoa and honey mixture until they are completely covered.

4. Place the bananas on a sheet of wax paper. Freeze them overnight. If you can't wait that long, freeze them for at least 3 hours.

SUPER WALL DECORATION

This is a good thing to make on a rainy day, when you have lots of time. Read all the instructions before you begin. If you don't have colored paper, use colorful pages from a magazine.

Here's what you need:

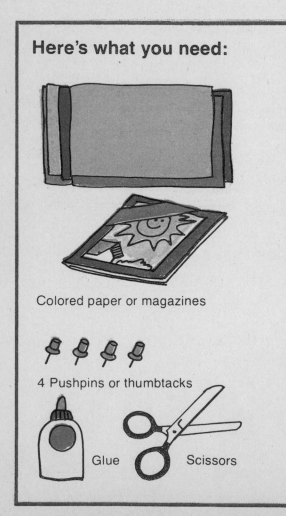

Colored paper or magazines

4 Pushpins or thumbtacks

Glue   Scissors

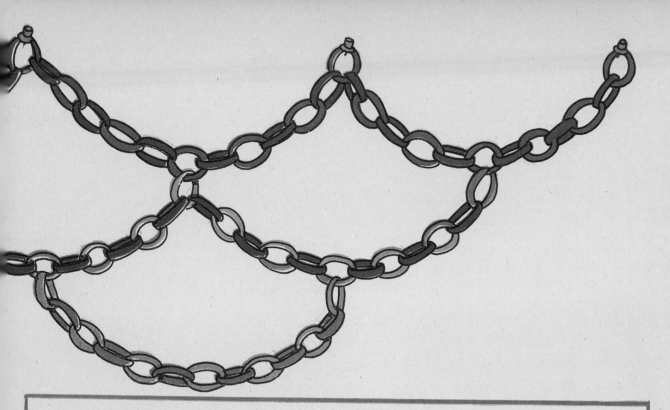

Here's what you do:

1 Cut 75 strips from colored paper to make 3 paper chains. You will need 37 strips for the longest chain. You will need 25 strips for the medium-length chain. You will need 13 strips for the shortest chain.

2 Make the chains by joining the strips together like this.

3 After you have your 3 chains, take the longest chain. Using pushpins, tack it to the wall as shown in the picture. It will be divided into 3 equal loops.

4 Take the medium-length chain and attach it to the longest chain as shown. It will be divided into 2 equal loops.

5 Take the shortest chain and attach it to the medium-length chain as shown. Now it's ready—at last!

CASTLE

Here's what you need:

Cardboard box

Cardboard tubes

Toothpick

Colored paper

Stiff, shiny ribbon

Felt-tip pens

Paper cup

Scissors

Cellophane Tape

Glue

Here's what you do:

1 Cut a piece of colored paper to fit around the box. Crease it where the corners are.

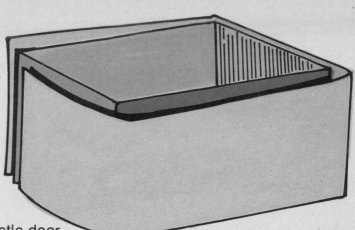

2 With a tan felt-tip pen, draw the stones of the castle walls. With the brown pen, make the castle door. With the black pen, add the windows and details of the castle door.

3 Glue the paper around the box. After the glue dries, cut notches along the top edges, as shown in the picture. To make the castle door open and close, cut around it along three sides.

4 Cover a cardboard tube with matching paper. Add stone pattern and windows. Cut notches in one end of the tube. This is the castle turret. Make two of these.

5 Glue the two turrets to opposite sides of the castle.

6 You can make a guard station from a small paper cup. Stand it next to the castle. Fly a banner from the top of the station.

7 Cut a piece of colored paper to fit around the cup. Draw stones, door, and window. Glue paper to cup. Cut a strip of stiff, shiny ribbon. Tape it to a toothpick. Stick the toothpick into the bottom of the paper cup. If you like, you can add a knight to stand alongside the guard station.

PERSONALIZED BARRETTE

Here's what you need:

Barrette

ALPHABET NOODLES

Alphabet noodles

Scissors

Glue

Colored paper

Paint and brush

Clear nail polish

Here's what you do:

1 Pick the letters of your name out of a box of alphabet noodles. Paint the letters any colors you like. After they dry, glue them to a barrette.

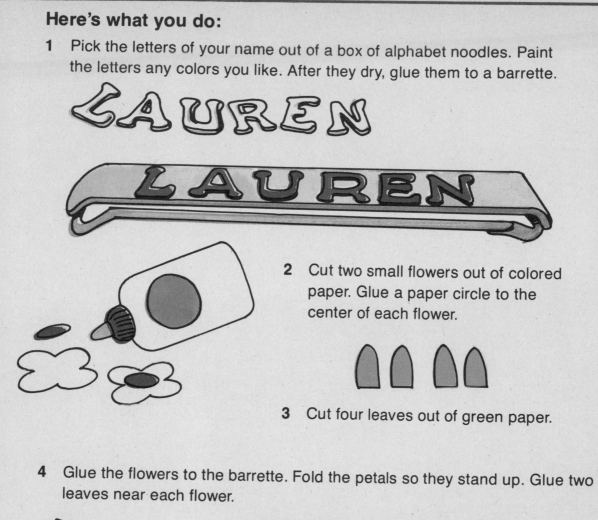

2 Cut two small flowers out of colored paper. Glue a paper circle to the center of each flower.

3 Cut four leaves out of green paper.

4 Glue the flowers to the barrette. Fold the petals so they stand up. Glue two leaves near each flower.

5 Brush a coat of clear nail polish on the letters, the flowers, and the leaves. Coat both sides of the petals and leaves.

6 After the polish is dry, brush on another coat. Wait 10 minutes. Then brush on a third coat.

PRETTY JARS AND BOTTLES

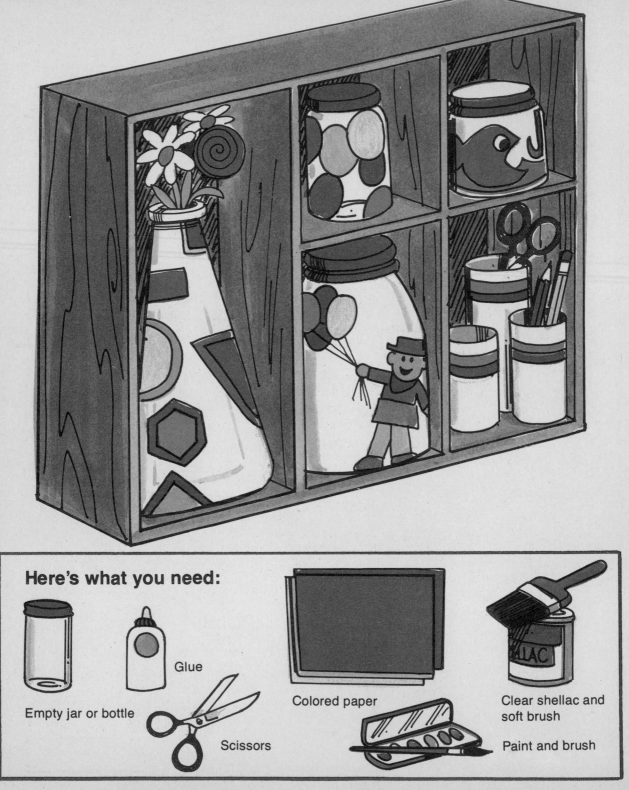

Here's what you need:

Empty jar or bottle

Glue

Scissors

Colored paper

Clear shellac and soft brush

Paint and brush

Here's what you do:

1   Choose a jar or bottle with a pretty shape. Make sure it is clean and dry.

2   Cut circles of many different sizes out of colored paper. Glue them to the jar or bottle.

3   Paint the jar's cover in a color to match.

4   When the paint and glue are dry, brush on a coat of clear shellac.

Other things you can do:

Decorate a small jar with a little paper fish and some waves. Add a fishhook. Glue all pieces to the jar; then shellac.

Decorate a mayonnaise jar with a balloon man and some paper balloons. Add pieces of string to hold the balloons. If you like, add a tree and some flowers. Use the jar for saving pennies.

Make a flower vase out of a long-necked bottle. Decorate it with tiny flowers or different sizes and shapes of colored paper.

Make a set of matching bottles and jars for your desk. Use them to hold pencils and paper clips.

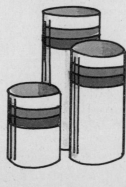

SOCK PUPPET

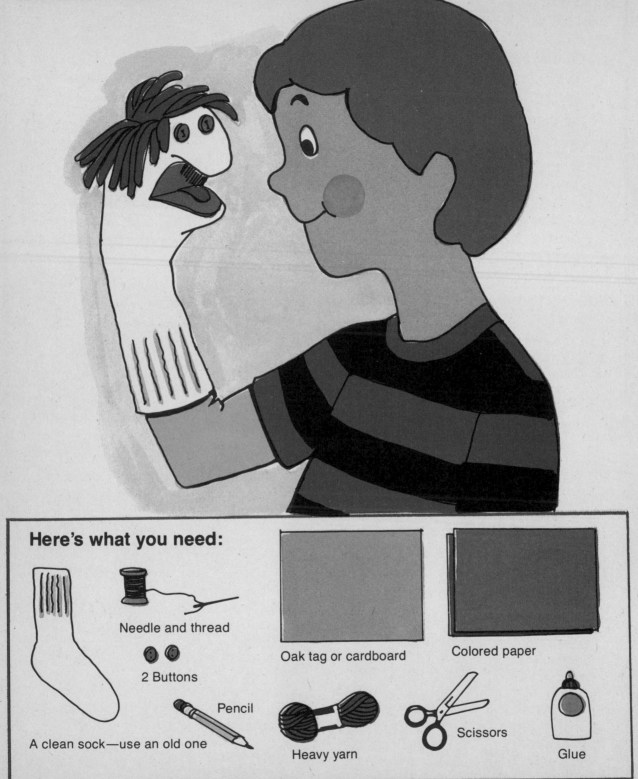

Here's what you need:

Needle and thread

2 Buttons

A clean sock—use an old one

Pencil

Heavy yarn

Oak tag or cardboard

Colored paper

Scissors

Glue

Here's what you do:

1 Cut the shape shown at right out of oak tag or cardboard. Glue it to a sheet of pink paper. Cut out around the oak tag. This is the puppet's mouth.

2 Cut out a tongue from red paper. Fold on dotted line and glue it to the center of the mouth.

3 Put the sock on your hand so your fingers are in the toe part and your thumb is in the heel.

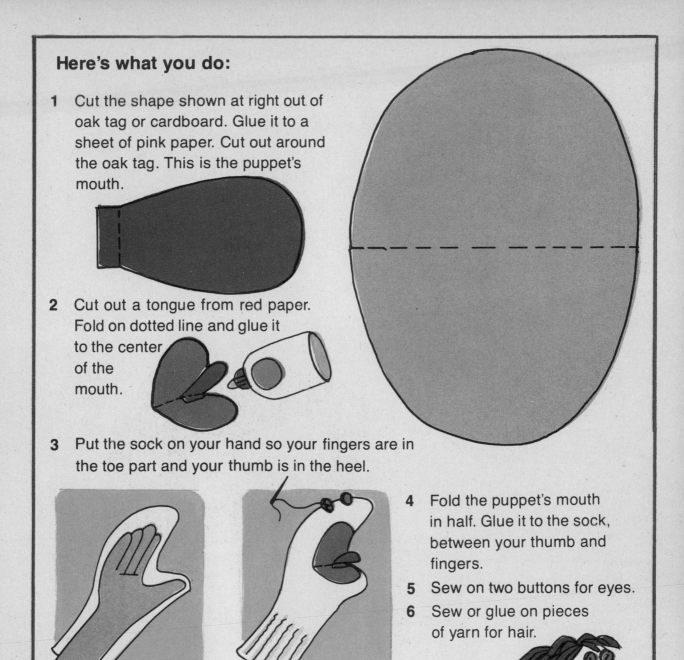

4 Fold the puppet's mouth in half. Glue it to the sock, between your thumb and fingers.

5 Sew on two buttons for eyes.

6 Sew or glue on pieces of yarn for hair.

You can also use strips of colored paper for hair. Curl the paper around a pencil, if you like curls.

Add a moustache made from paper or yarn. Add earrings. Add a bow. Use a green sock to make a frog. Add a long tongue and some frog's spots cut from black paper.

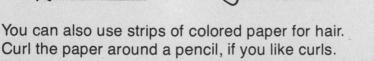

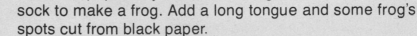

YUM YUMS

If you are not allowed to use the oven by yourself, ask a grownup for help.

Here's what you need:

Stick of butter or margarine

1½ Cups graham-cracker crumbs

12 Ounces semisweet chocolate bits

6 Ounces butterscotch bits

Wooden spoon

Pot holders

Small can of sweetened condensed milk

Baking pan, about 13" x 9"

Here's what you do:

1 Set the oven at 350°

2 Put a stick of butter or margarine in a baking pan. Place the pan in the oven.

When the butter melts, take the pan out of the oven. *Remember to use a pot holder!*

3 Pour the graham-cracker crumbs into the pan of butter. Stir with a wooden spoon until the crumbs are coated with butter. Press the crumbs down with your fingers, so they cover the bottom of the pan.

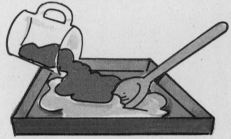

4 Sprinkle half of the chocolate bits over the crumbs. Sprinkle the butterscotch bits on top. Then sprinkle the rest of the chocolate bits.

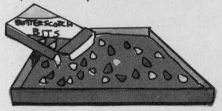

5 Pour the sweetened condensed milk over the mixture. Pour it evenly. Cover as much of the pan as you can.

6 Bake everything for 20 to 25 minutes or until the top is golden brown and slightly bubbly.

7 Using a pot holder, take the pan out of the oven.

8 Let the Yum Yums cool for a while, then cut them into squares—*Yum Yum!*

DESIGN YOUR OWN T-SHIRT

(*Note:* If you are not allowed to use an iron by yourself, ask a grownup for help.)

Here's what you need:

T-shirt

Iron-on crayons
(buy them in a craft or hobby store)

Paper

Pins

Pencil

Iron

Ironing board

Here's what you do:

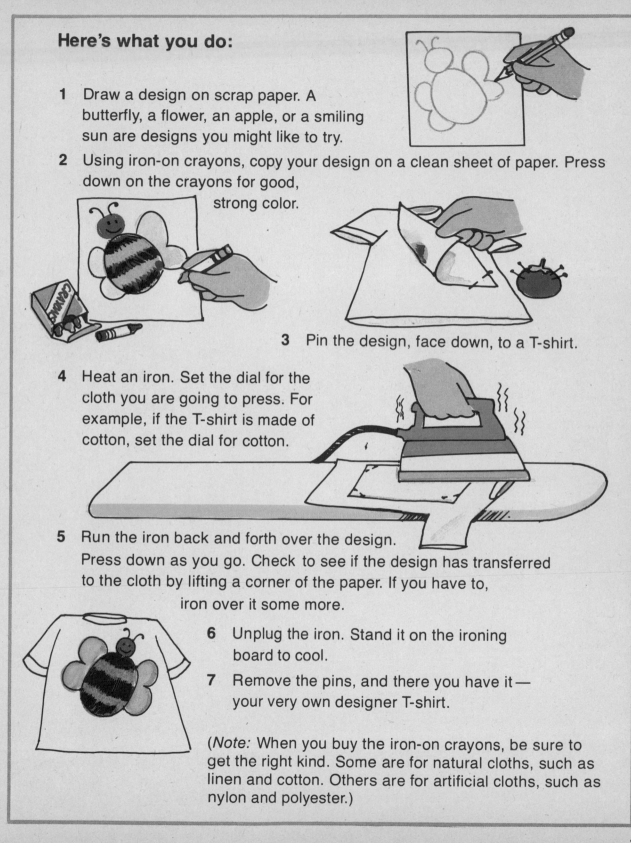

1 Draw a design on scrap paper. A butterfly, a flower, an apple, or a smiling sun are designs you might like to try.

2 Using iron-on crayons, copy your design on a clean sheet of paper. Press down on the crayons for good, strong color.

3 Pin the design, face down, to a T-shirt.

4 Heat an iron. Set the dial for the cloth you are going to press. For example, if the T-shirt is made of cotton, set the dial for cotton.

5 Run the iron back and forth over the design. Press down as you go. Check to see if the design has transferred to the cloth by lifting a corner of the paper. If you have to, iron over it some more.

6 Unplug the iron. Stand it on the ironing board to cool.

7 Remove the pins, and there you have it — your very own designer T-shirt.

(*Note:* When you buy the iron-on crayons, be sure to get the right kind. Some are for natural cloths, such as linen and cotton. Others are for artificial cloths, such as nylon and polyester.)

SUPERBALL

Look! Up in the sky!
It's a ball!
It's super!
It's *Superball!*

Here's what you need:

A jack

Lots of rubber bands

Here's what you do:

1 Loop a rubber band around a jack. Twist the rubber band and loop it around again. Do this until all of the rubber band is twisted tightly around the jack.

2 Add another rubber band the same way.

3 Keep adding rubber bands until the jack is completely covered.

Your Superball can be as big as you like. Just add more rubber bands and watch it grow! Now bounce the *Superball*— there it goes!

DANCING CLOWN

Here's what you need:

Colored paper

Scissors

Glue

Cellophane tape

Pencil

3 Rubber bands

Black, orange, and blue felt-tip pens

44

Here's what you do:

1 Use the patterns on the next two pages. Cut out the clown's head from white paper. Add orange eyebrows. Draw two eyes.

2 Cut out a red nose and a pink mouth. Glue in place.

3 Cut out two orange-colored shapes for the hair. Curl the ends around a pencil. Glue a fringe of hair to each side of the clown's head.

4 To make the collar, fold a white circle in half. Fold it in half again and again. Snip the tip off. Open the circle and then fold it like an accordion. Open it again and add a blue stripe around the edge.

5 To make the pants, fold a piece of colored paper in half. Cut out half a heart shape. Unfold the heart. Tape or glue it to the back of the collar.

6 Cut out a red triangle and a round yellow tassel for the hat. Glue the tassel to the hat. Glue the hat to the clown's head. Glue the head to the collar.

7 Cut out two white gloves and two blue shoes.

8 Cut two rubber bands in half. Cut the other rubber band in only one place to open it up.

9 Tape the long rubber band to the clown's head.

10 Tape one end of each short rubber band to the back of each shoe. Tape the other ends to the back of the pants.

11 Tape the remaining cut rubber bands to the gloves and tape the other ends to the underside of the collar.

12 Add a pink circle to the front of the clown's pants. Using a black felt-tip pen, add a smile to the clown's mouth.

13 Hold the clown by the rubber band that comes from his head. Now you can make the clown dance!

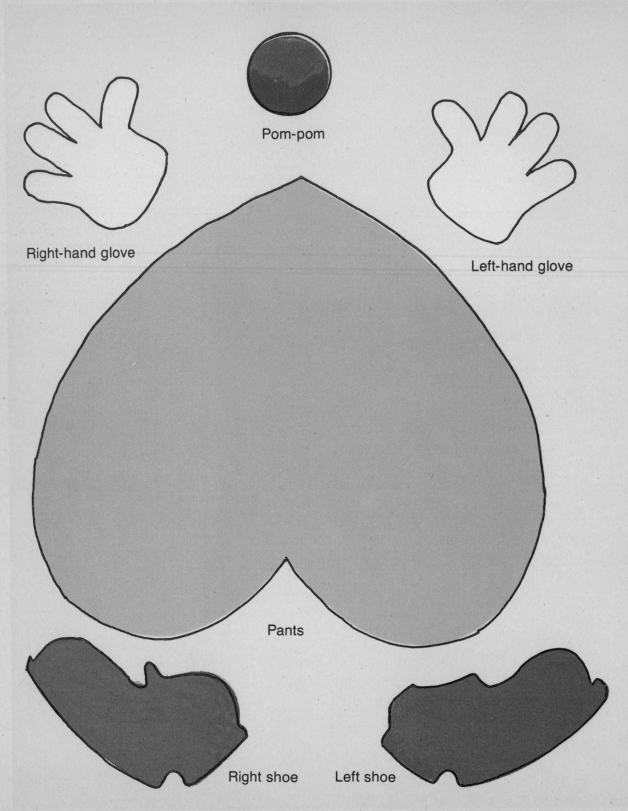

Pom-pom

Right-hand glove

Left-hand glove

Pants

Right shoe

Left shoe

46

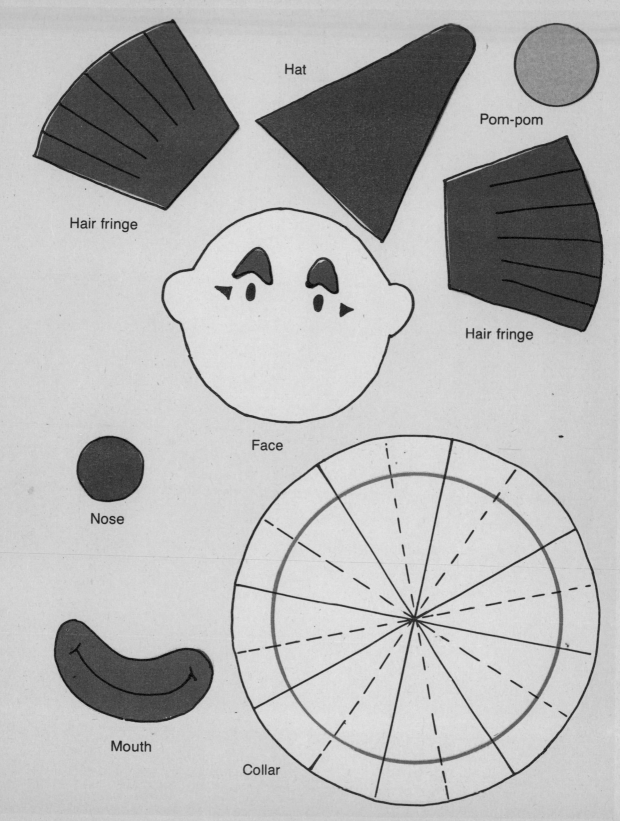

Hat

Pom-pom

Hair fringe

Hair fringe

Face

Nose

Mouth

Collar